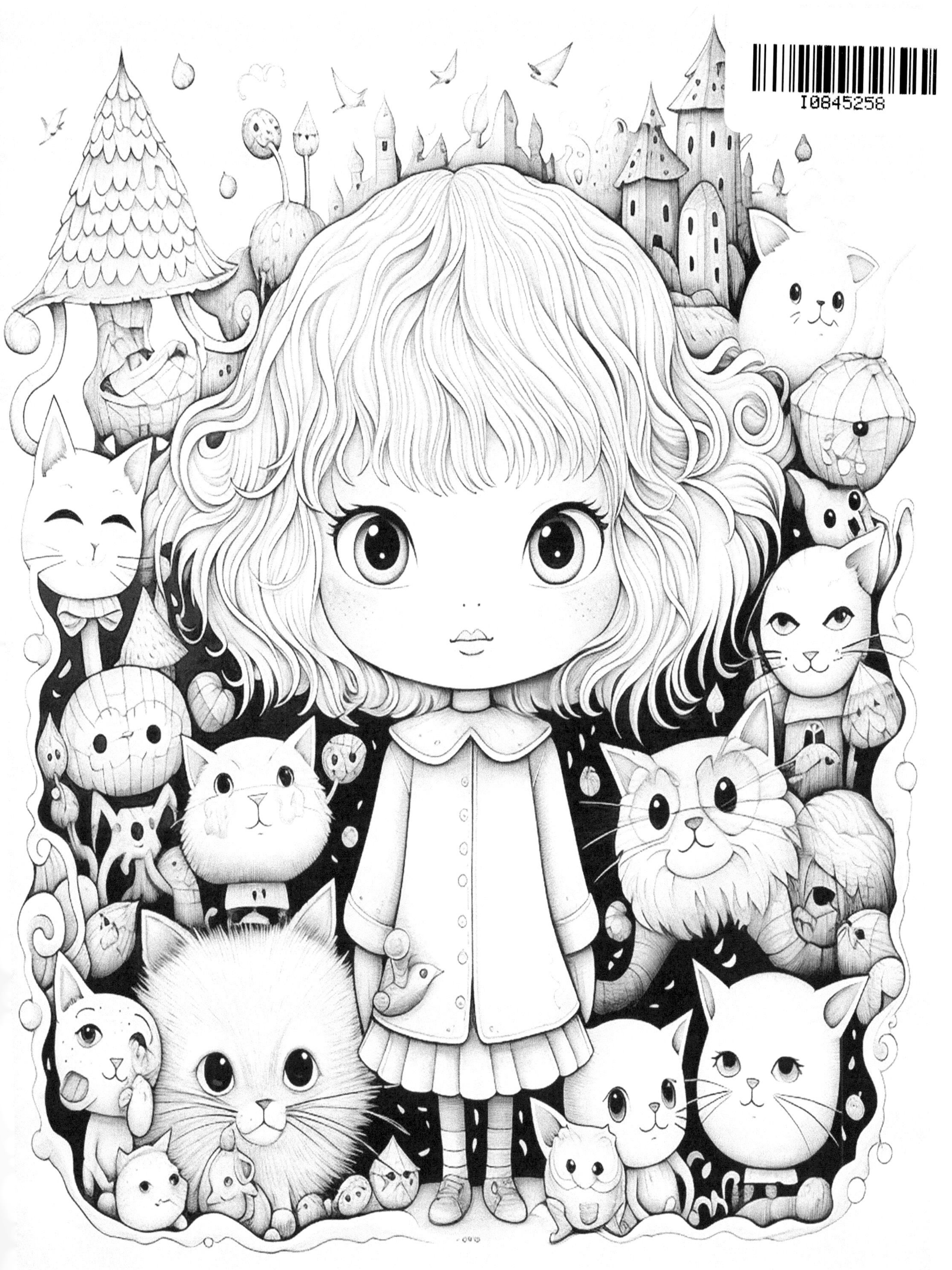
I0845258

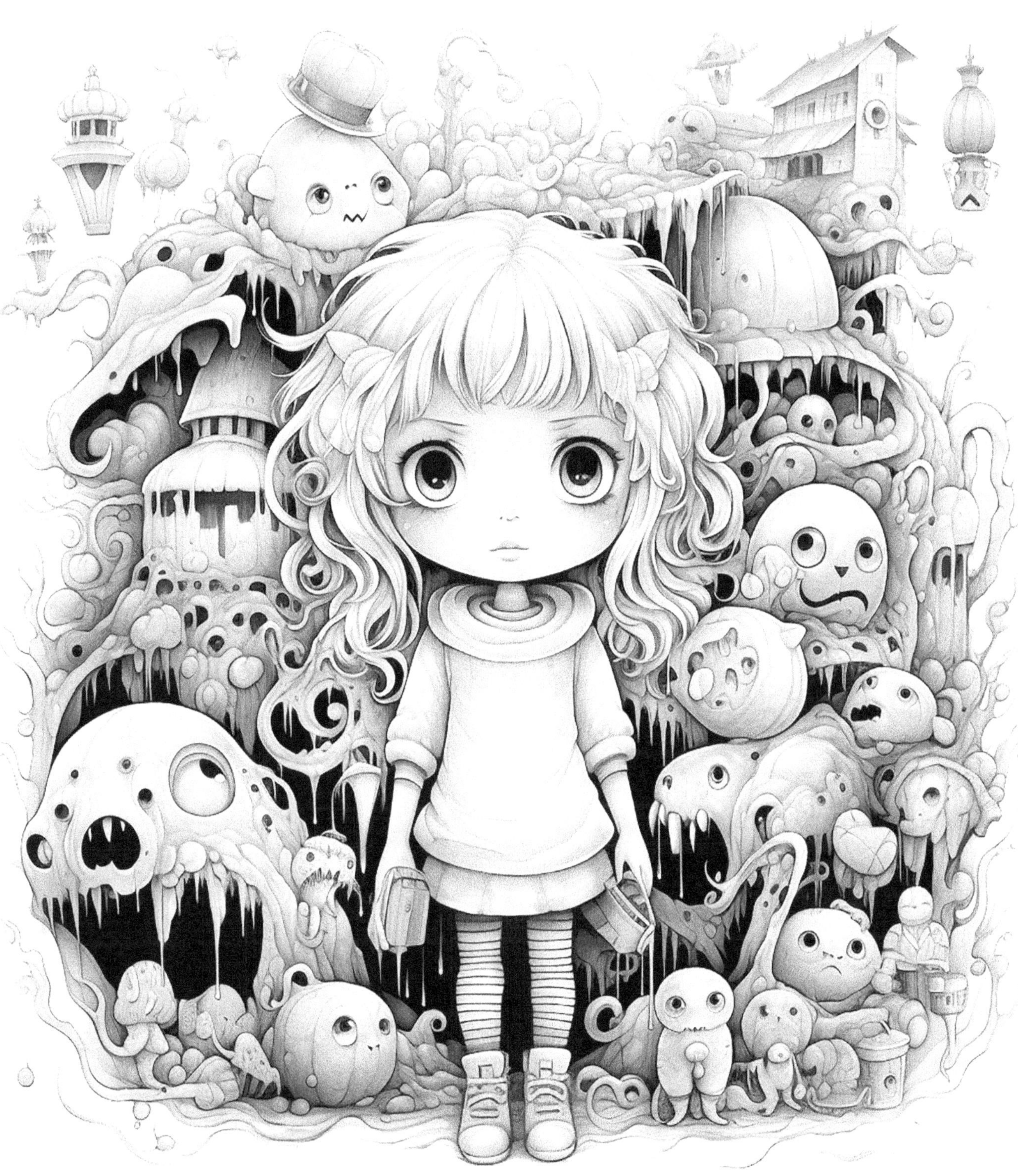

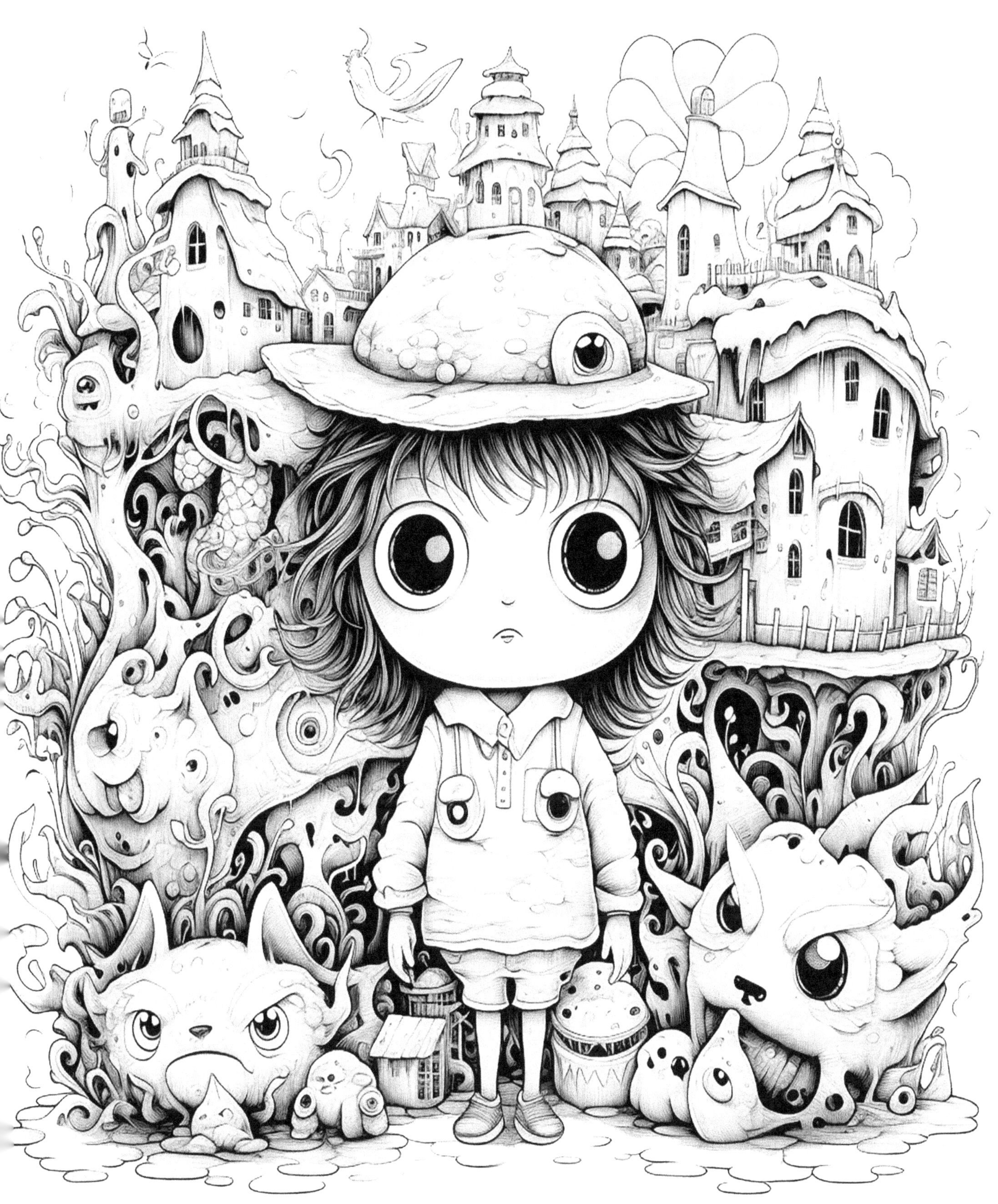

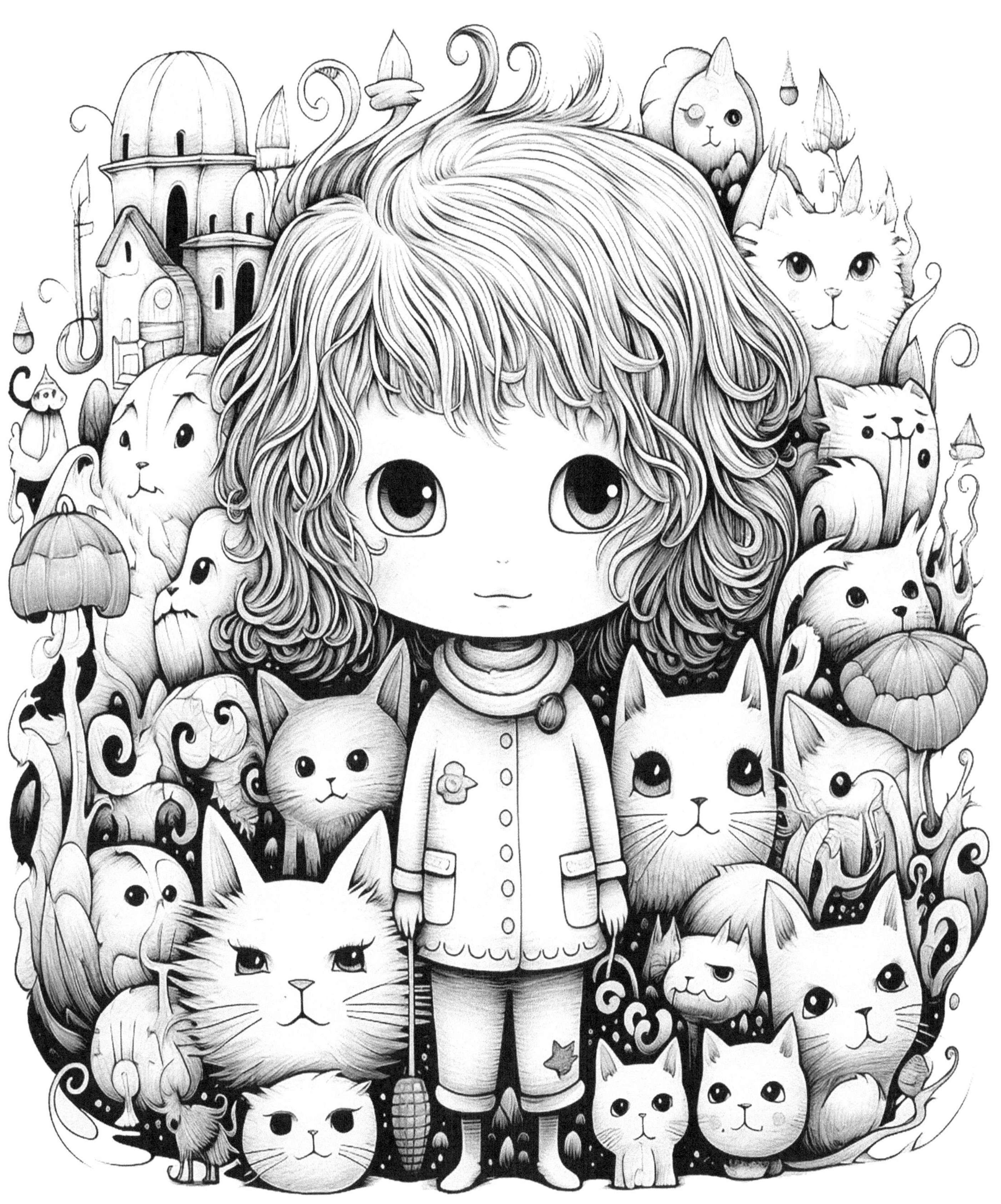

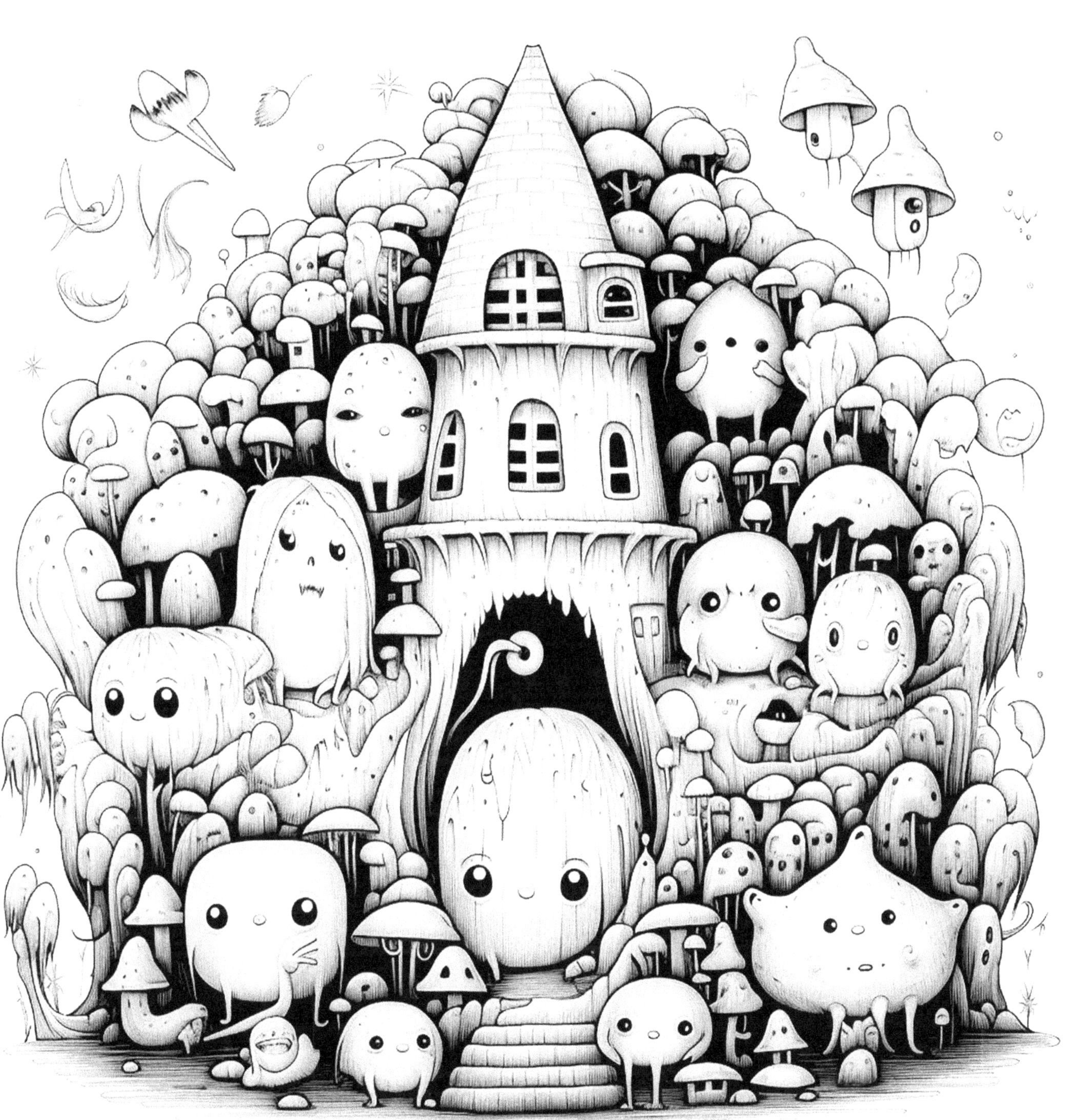

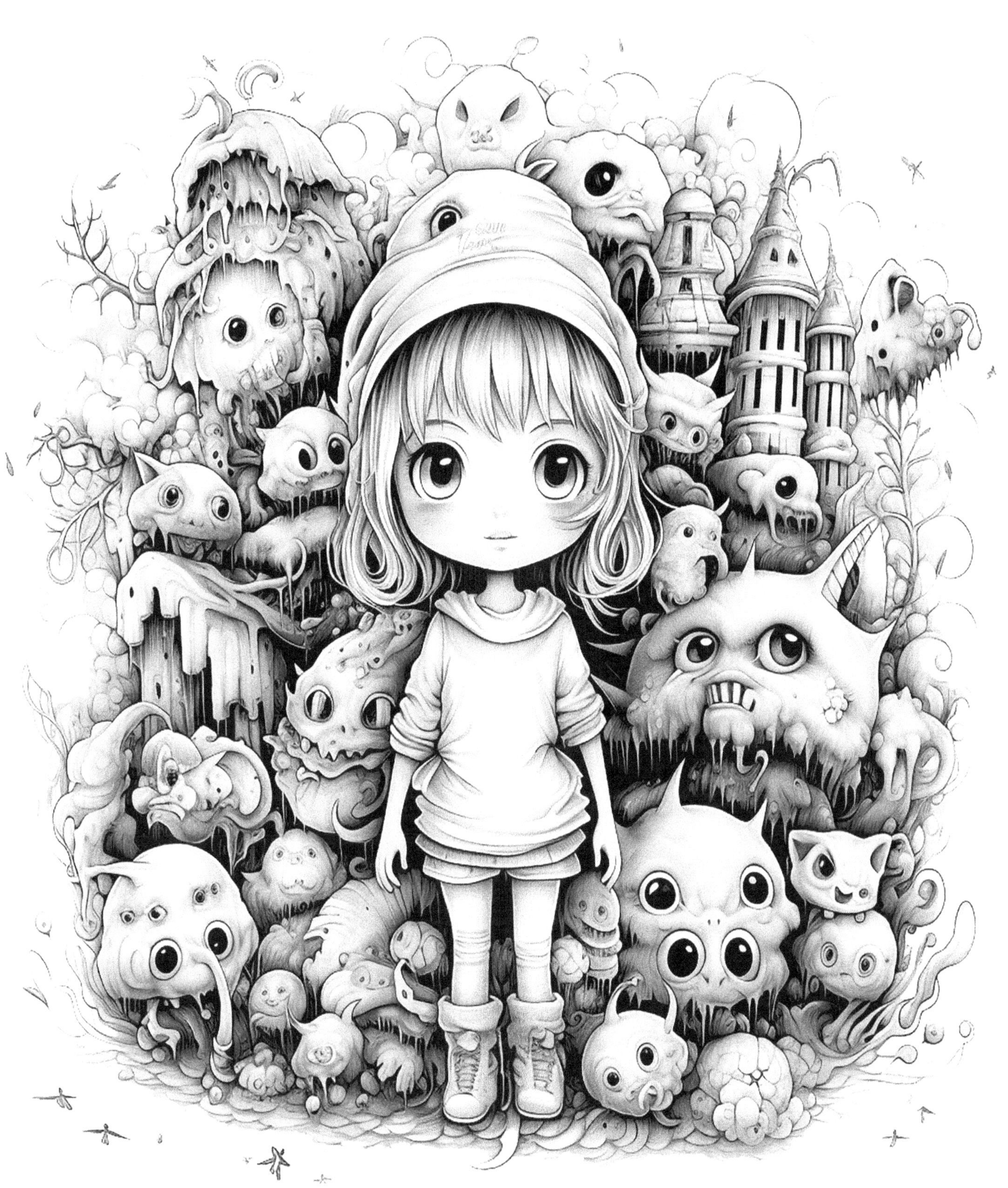

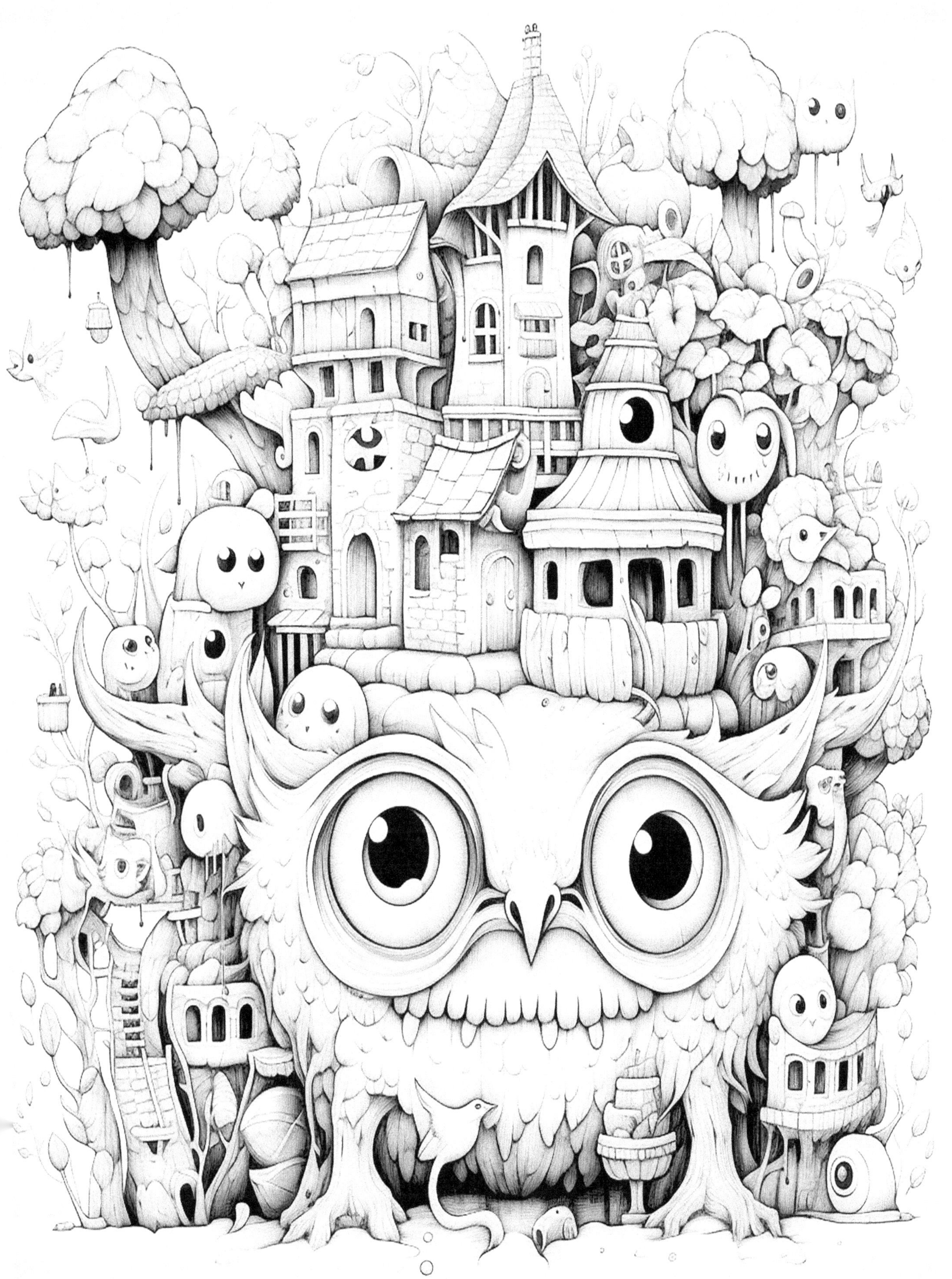

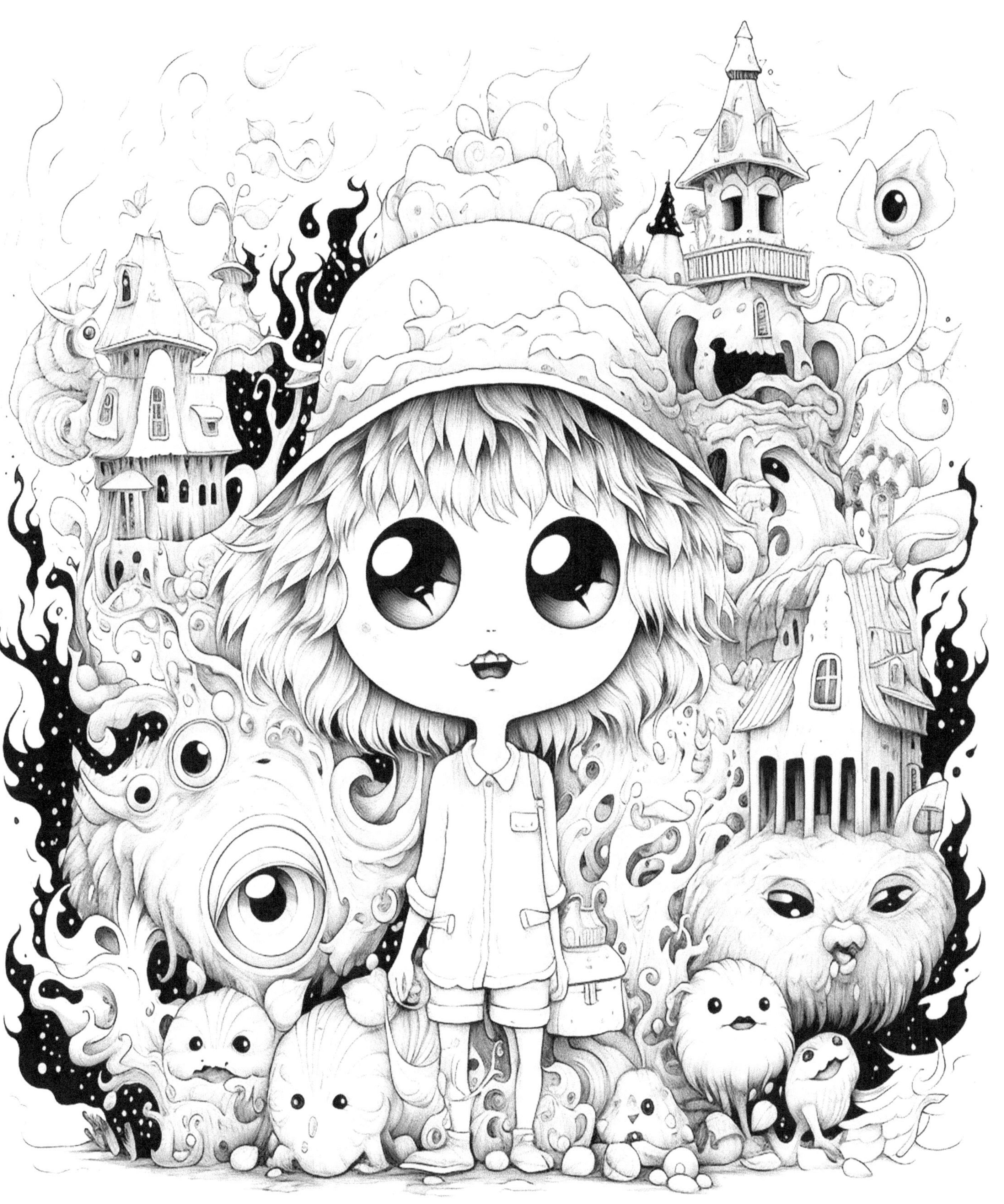

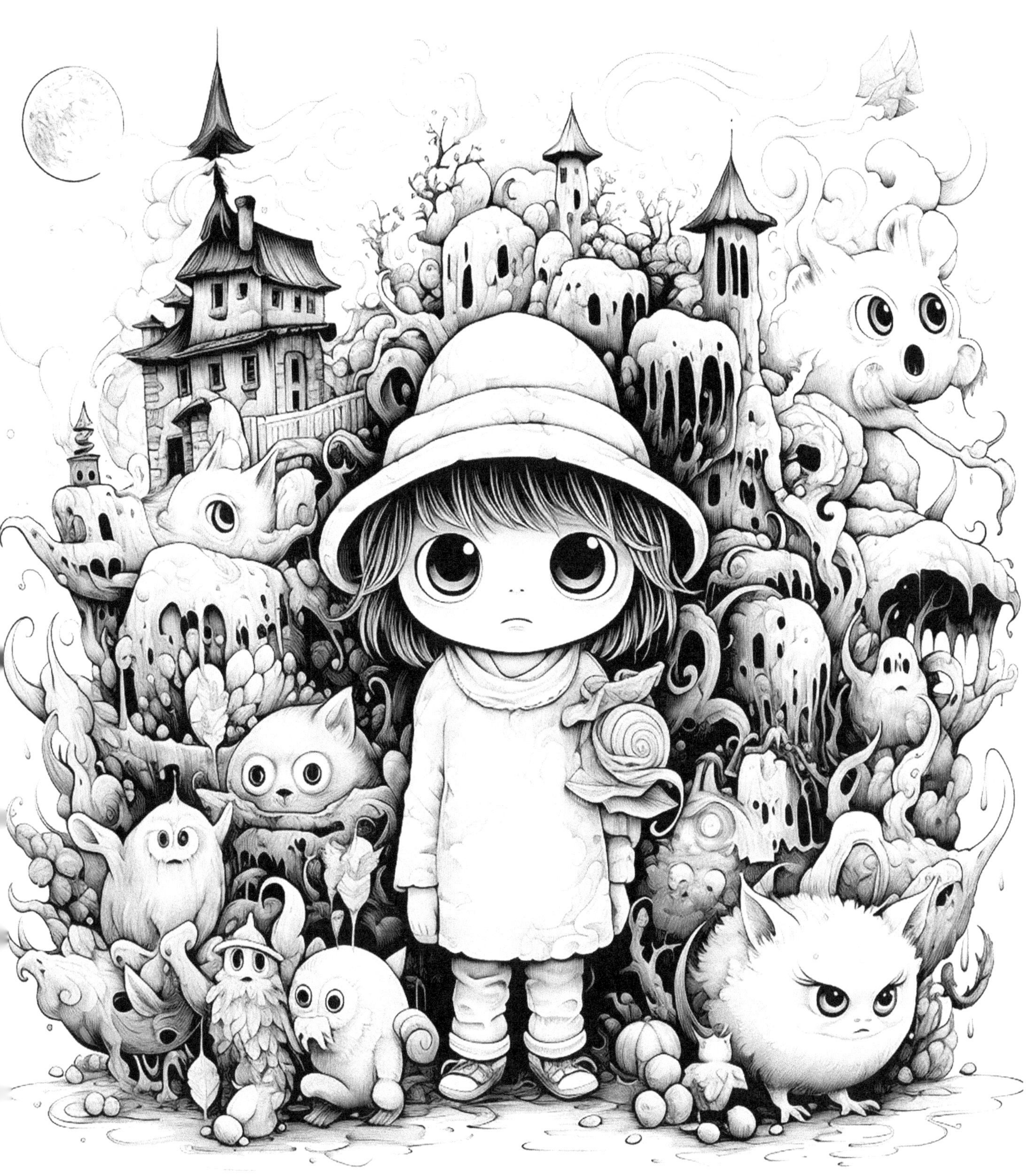

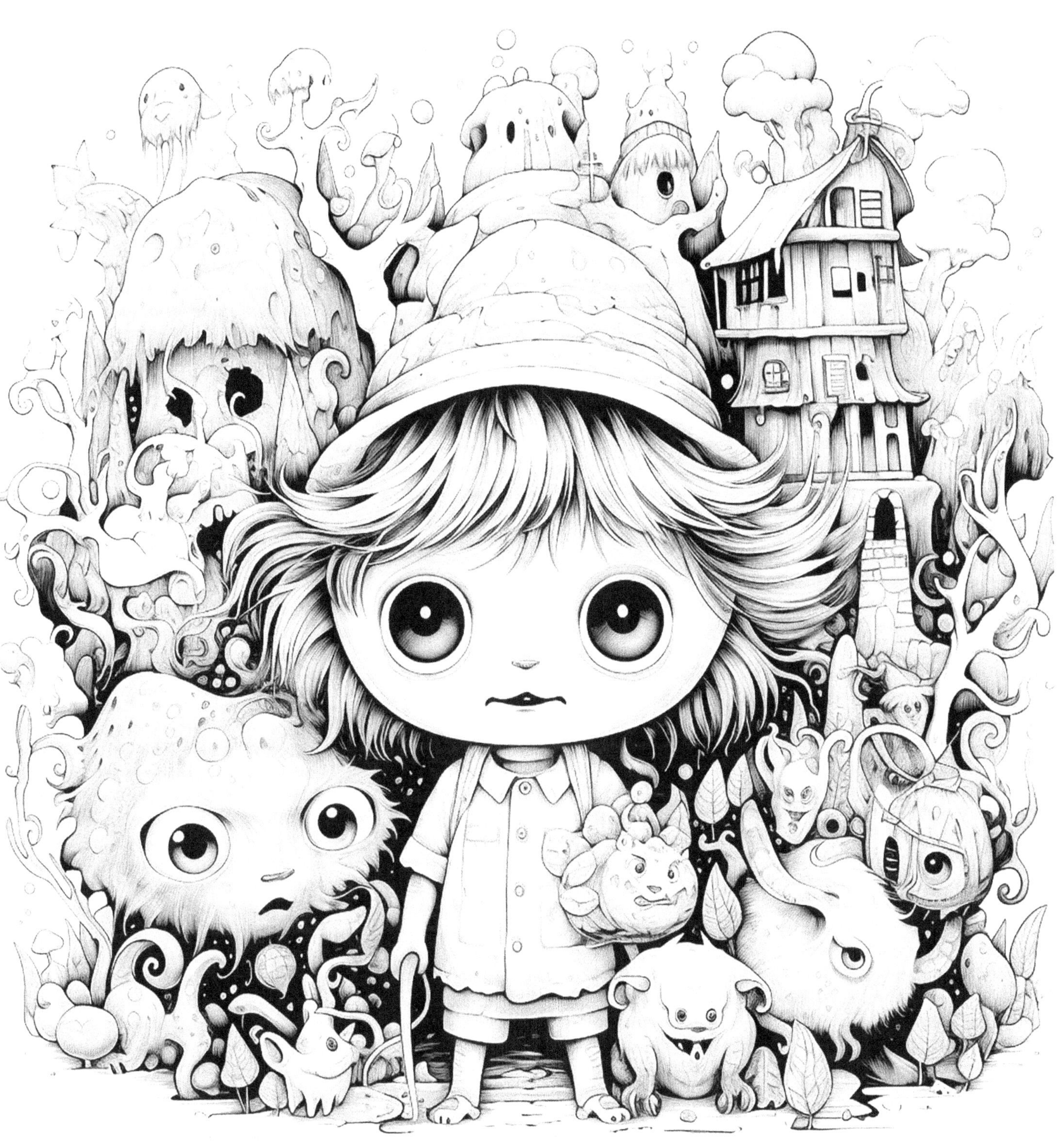

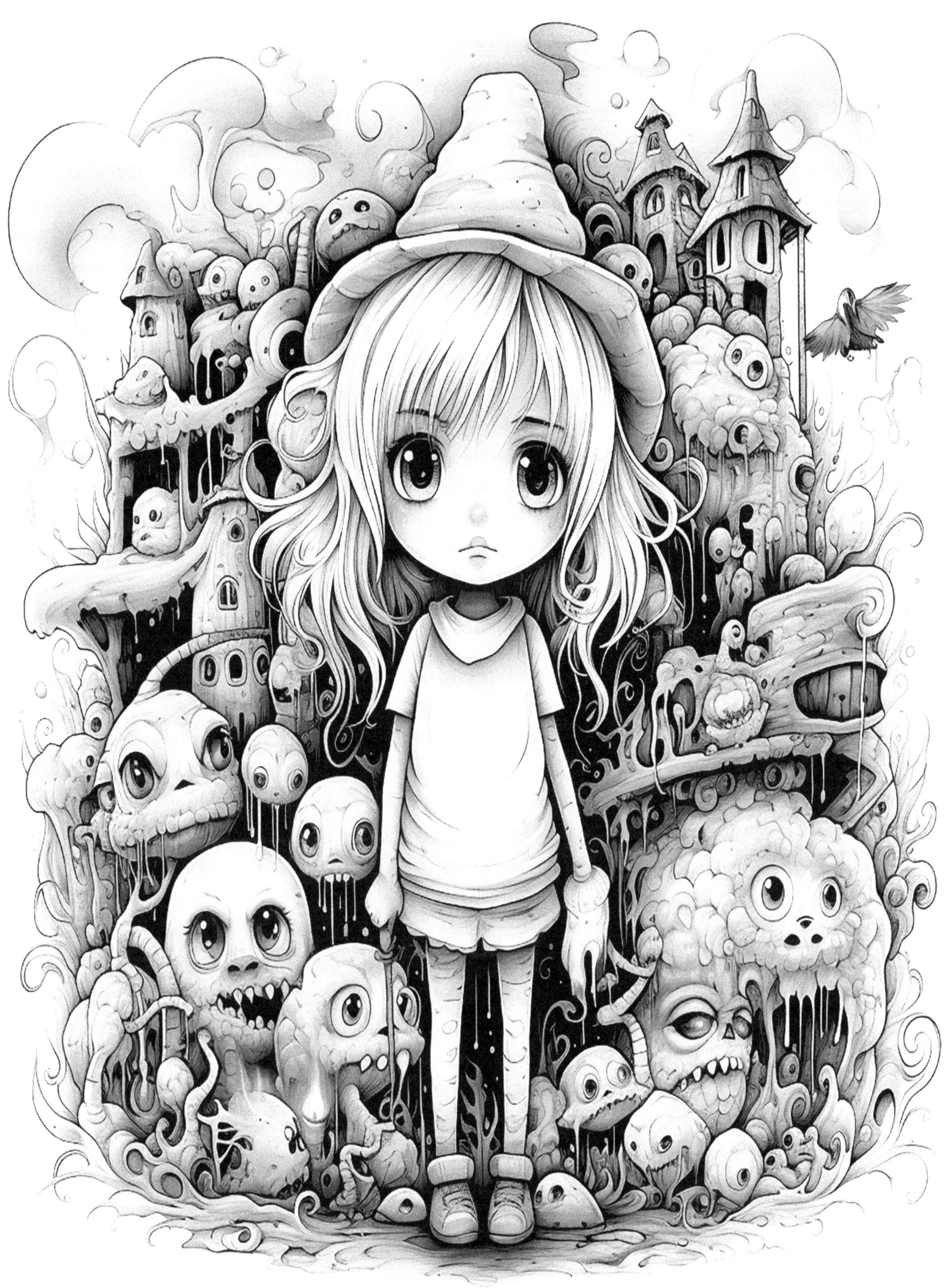

TESTIMONIALS

EDWARD STEVENSON, COMMUNITY LEADER, KANSAS CITY

The writers of the pieces in the "Hope Stories" are exceptional young people.
I have not met them physically. I have only (only?!?!) known them through their writings. Their personal maturity is exceptional. Their experiences are exceptionally fraught in ways most of us, thank goodness, have never known. In many cases the very writing itself is exceptional. And in all that I have read there is an exceptional commitment, an exceptional discipline, an exceptional persistence in seeking hope even in the midst of terrifyingly threatening circumstances.

We are in a time when too, too many of the world's leaders and peoples seem bent on violence, when nature itself seems to be becoming more and more hostile to human well-being, when many even among those who are economically and socially comfortable seem to be turning to tantalizing distractions or simply falling into depression and despair. By contrast these young writers are heroes and should be recognized as psychological, spiritual and moral leaders.

The reason is that they demonstrate a commitment to building and maintaining hope and meaning in the midst of extreme circumstances. Circumstances of sudden, unwarranted arrest and denial of due process of law; circumstances of physical abuse and even outright torture; circumstances of isolation from family and loved ones; circumstances of imprisonment and ongoing verbal and psychological harassment by those who are supposed to be the upholders of justice.

Read these stories. Sense their courage. Observe a maturity that seems far beyond their youthfulness. Then examine your own commitments to justice, to a freedom beyond mere physical and social circumstance. As it has for me, let their hope inspire, enlarge and even strengthen your own.

BONNIE HAGHIRIAN

"I donated to AST because I am a mother. I cannot imagine having my child confined in a prison, away from family, away from life itself. I donated to AST because I have a voice, and those who are silenced have none. When one of us is hurting, we all are hurting."

JAMIE FRAZIER

"We have watched Turkey devolve from an open, multicultural society into an autocracy that imprisons and tortures those who share different opinions or are identified with any group the government deems as threatening. It breaks our hearts that families and friends are separated and suffering only because they seek peace and understanding."

EYYUP ESEN

"I have been volunteering for AST to be the voice of babies/kids and oppressed women and men. AST is the hope of desperate people in Turkey. They are the light at the end of the Turkish tunnel. Please donate so that their fight for freedom and justice can continue."

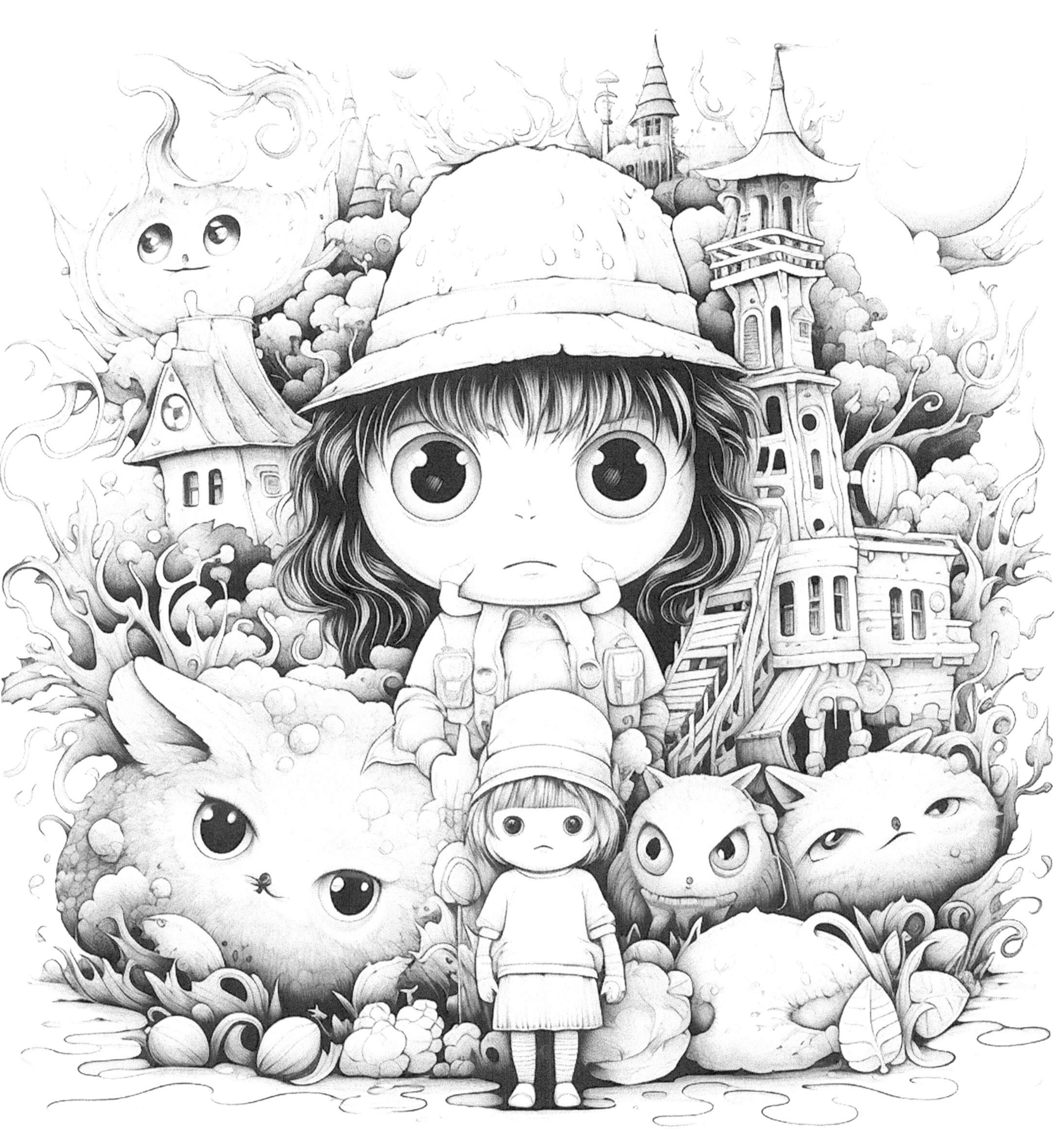

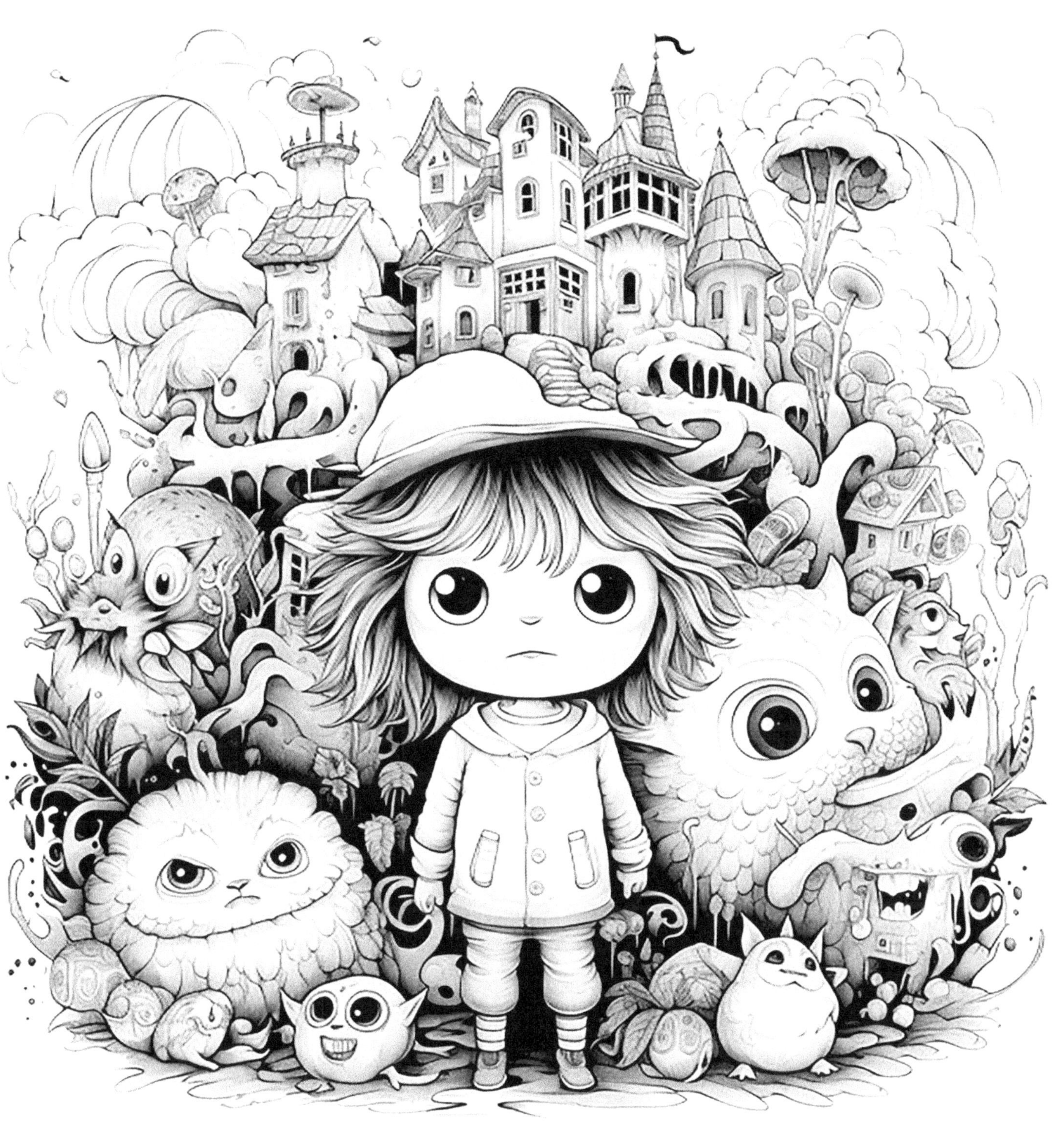

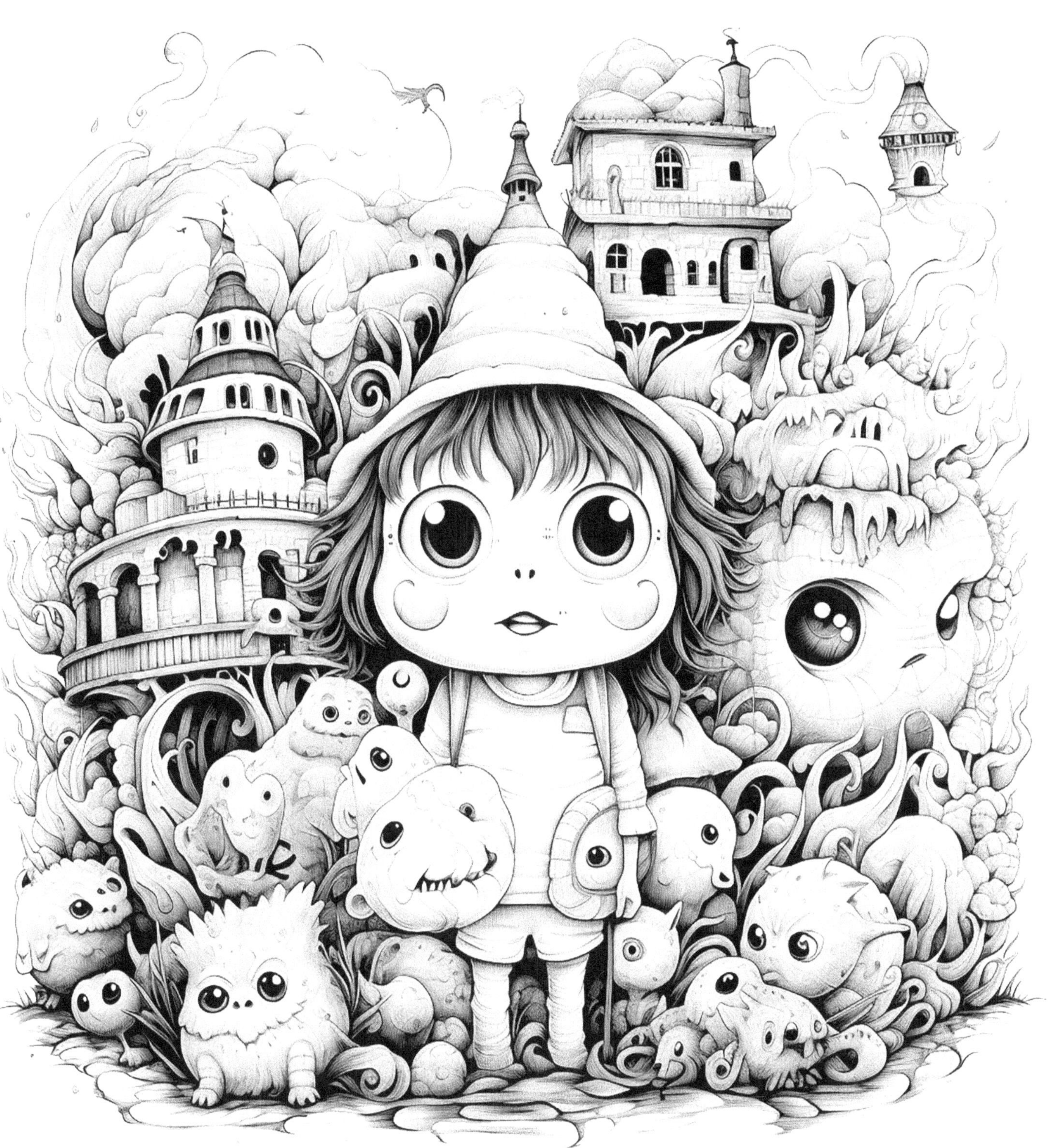

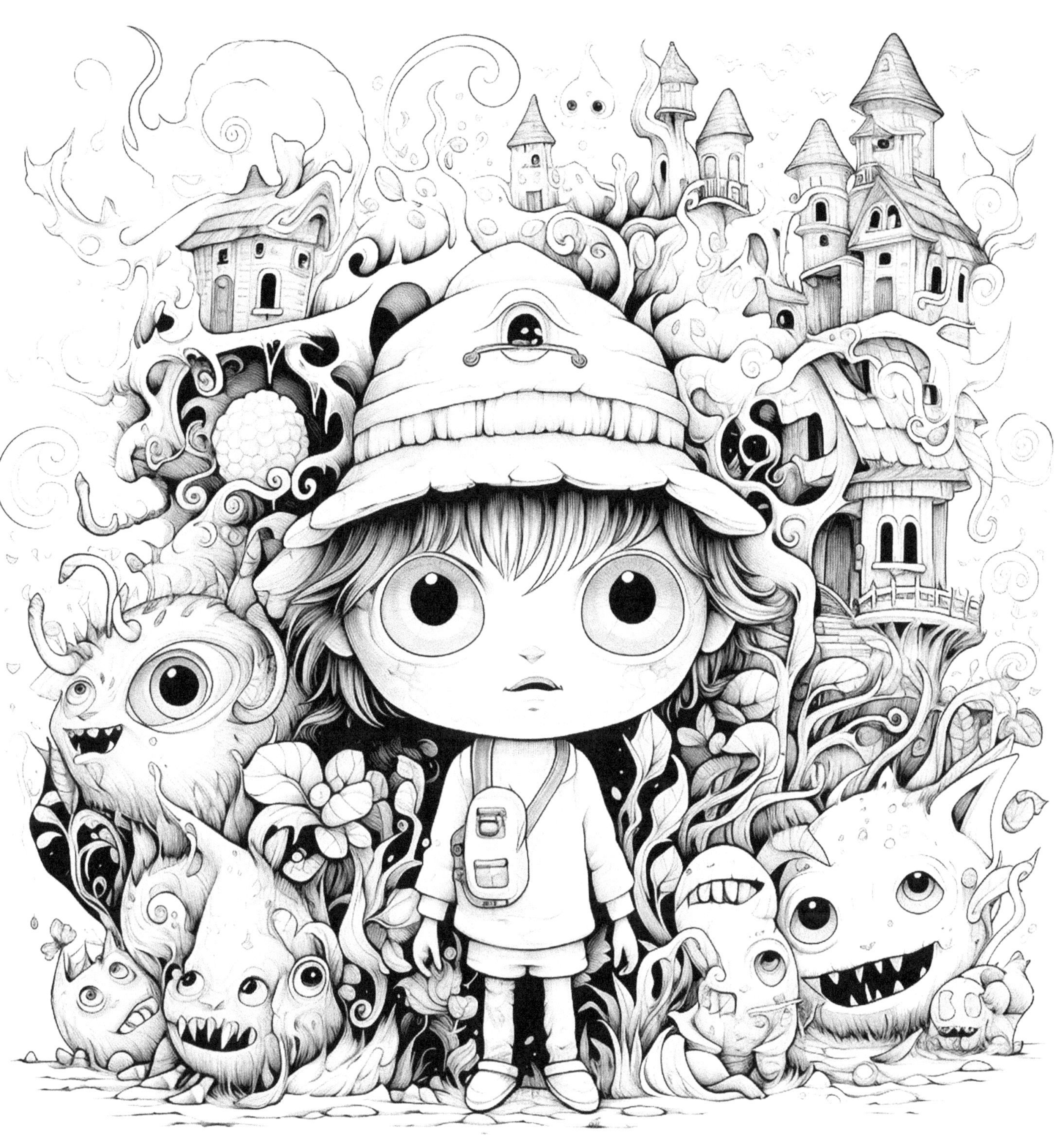

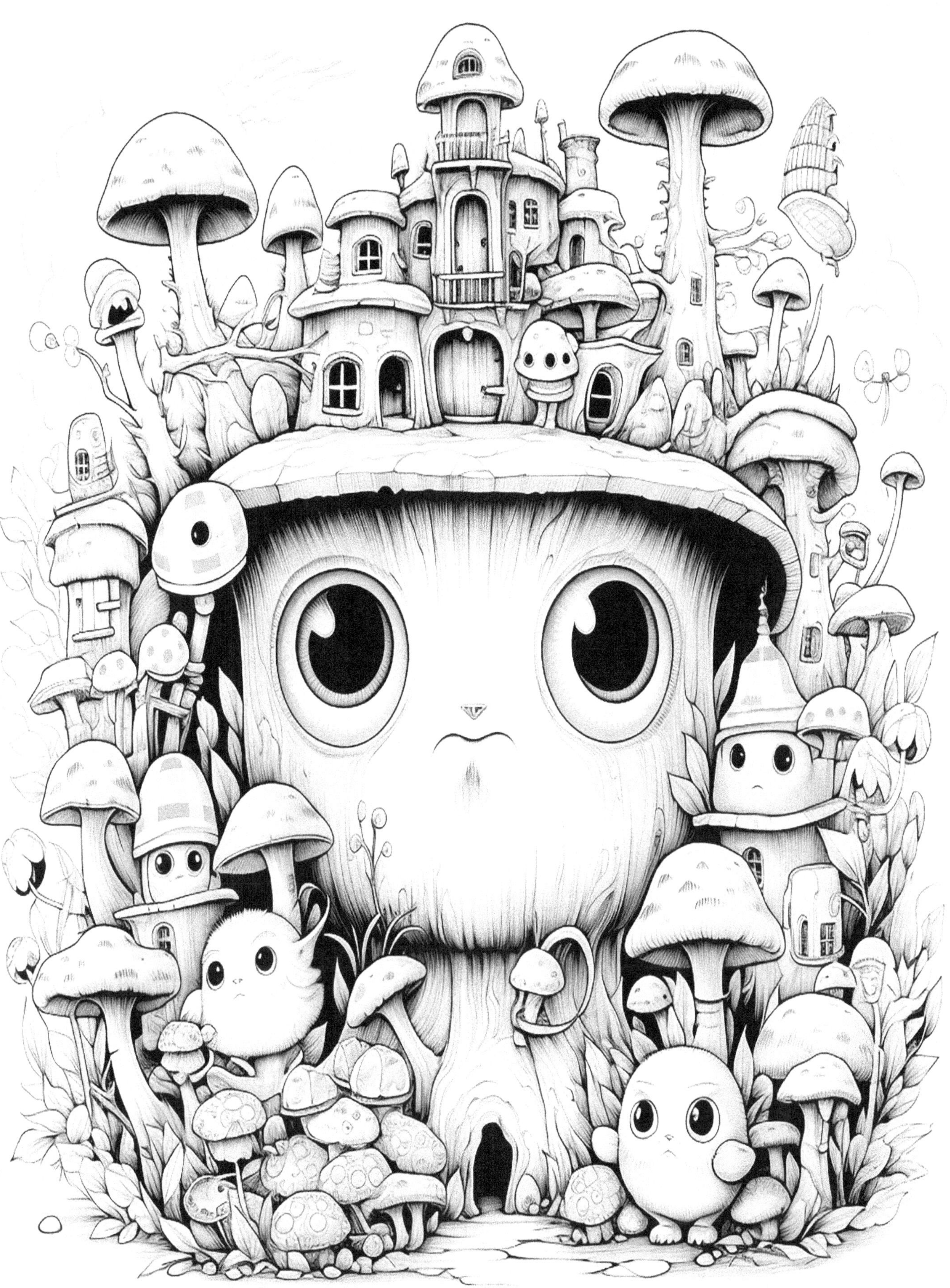

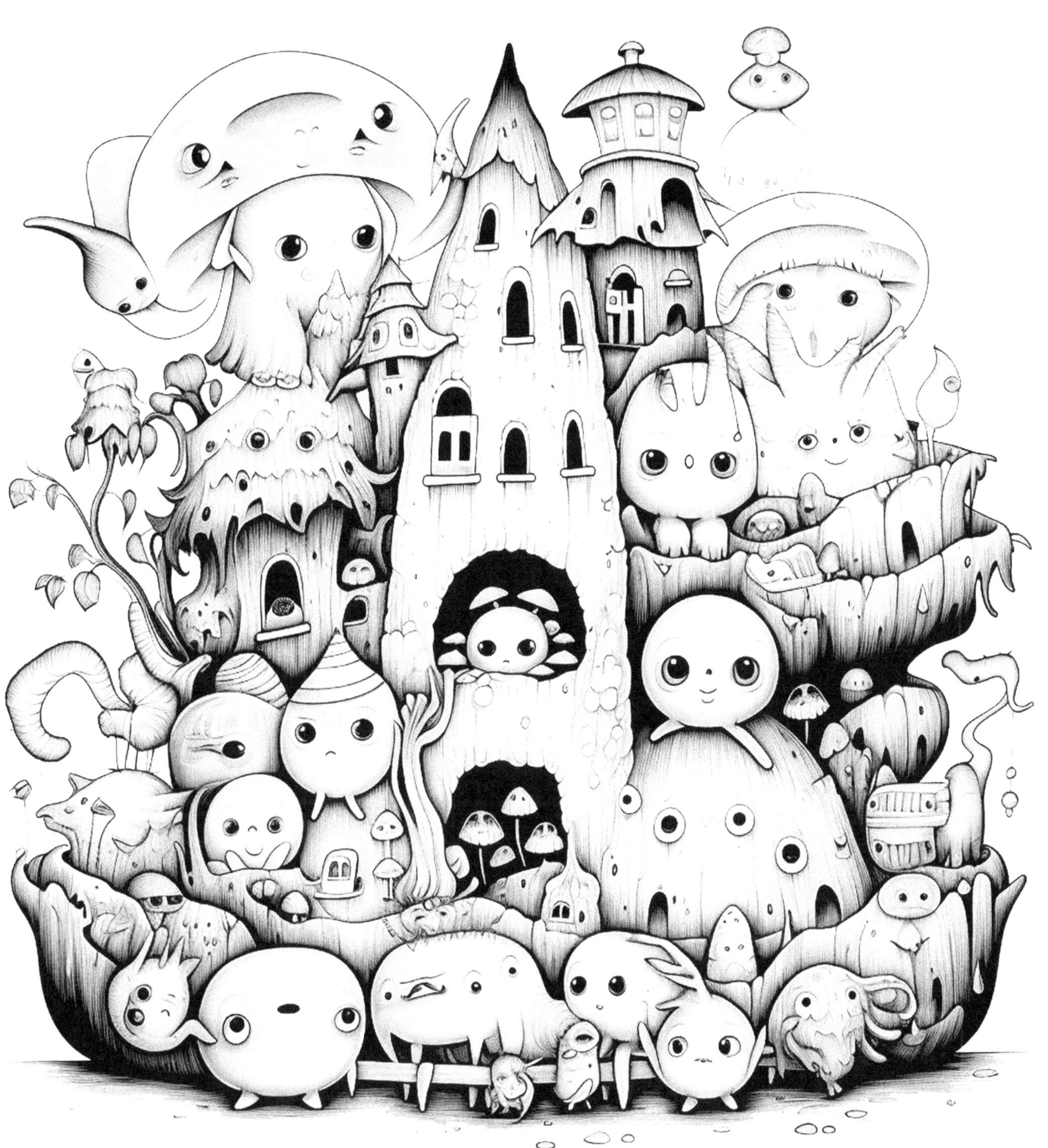

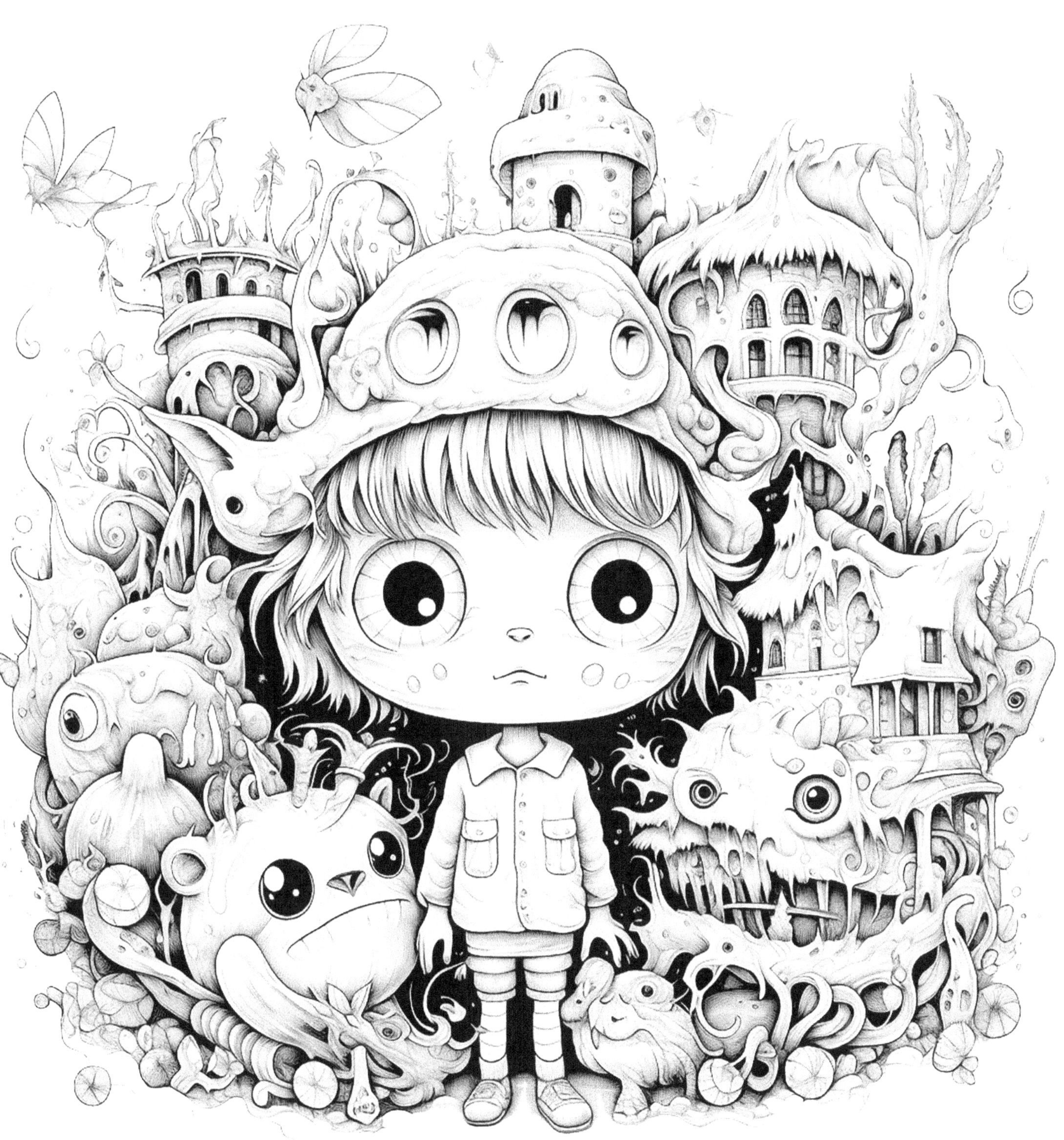

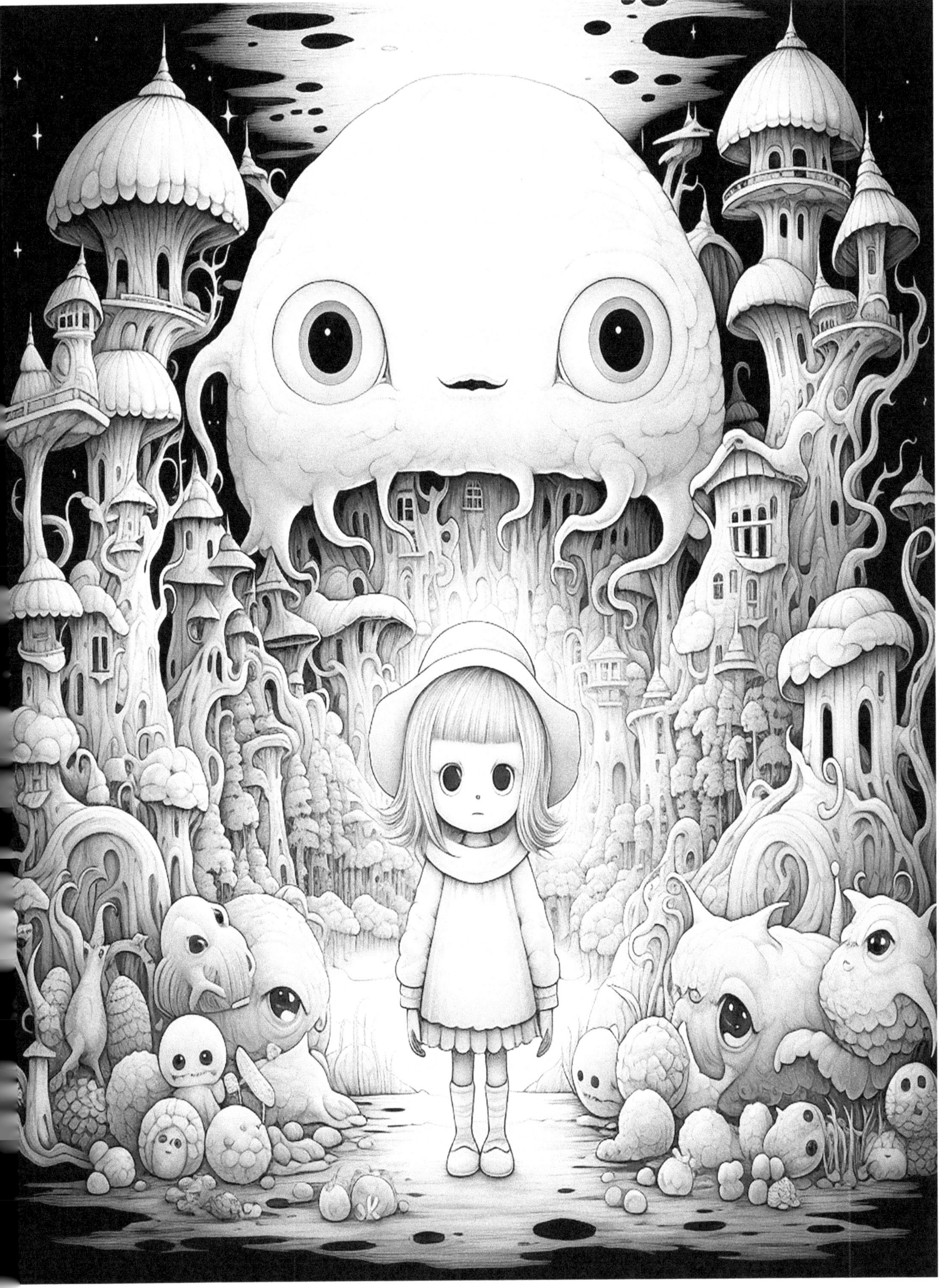